Wisdom Speaks

Hardcover ISBN: 978-1-0879-0093-3
Paperback ISBN: 979-8-52116-353-3

A Publication of *Tall Pine Books*
tallpinebooks.com

*Published in the United States of America

Wisdom Speaks

Practical insight for everyday life

J Norbert McDaniel

Don't reinvent the wheel...

...use it more *effectively*.

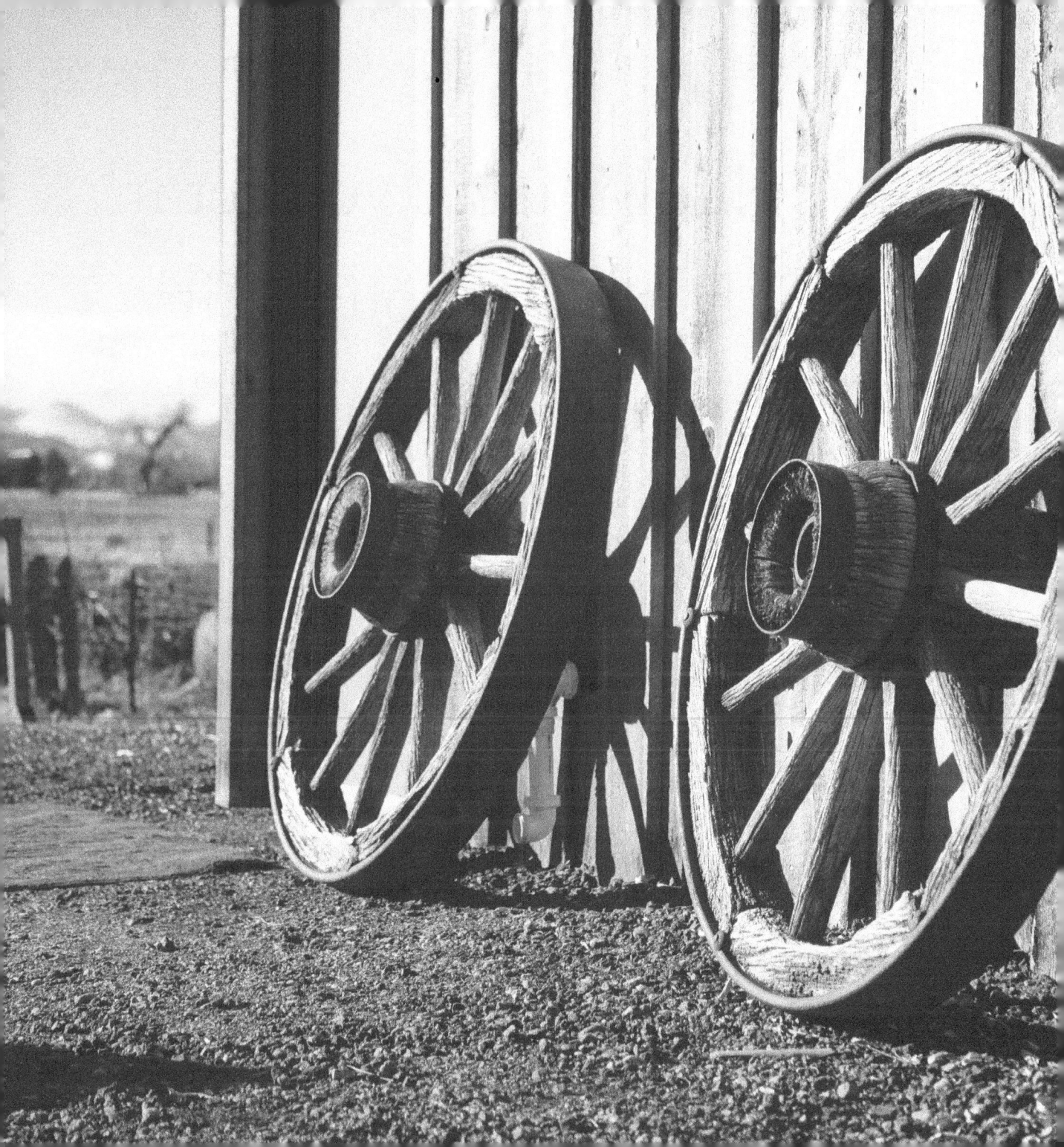

REACH for it until you get it!

BELIEVE it until you see it!

SAY it until you have it!

YOU MANAGE YOUR *time* BY MANAGING YOUR *desires.*

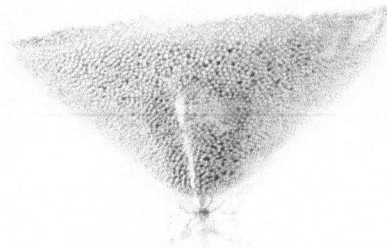

Great ideas and great people develop great service for others by improving the quality of life.

LOVE PRESENTS YOU WITH A POWERFUL REASON AND OPPORTUNITY TO *CHANGE.*

"And over all these virtues put on love, which binds them all together in perfect unity." Colossians 3:14

pleased... best,
gone to rest
heard the tale,
s might all,
homas,
cholas.

He comb his
by so-begens
He sang
He sent
And

He lay her
For in
And for

If you focus on your mistakes it will hold you captive.

If you <u>review</u> your mistakes you can improve your future decisions.

What you learn from
a wise person is more
important than what they
can pay you.

Information is more valuable than money. And to increase in *wisdom* is more valuable to your soul, than a fool finding gold.

ONLY IN <u>COMMITMENT</u> DO YOU SUCCEED.

UNTIL YOU *DO* WHAT YOU *SAY*...

WHAT YOU *SAY* HAS *NO* MEANING.

You may know who loves you, not only by the words they say, but also by their commitment to your future.

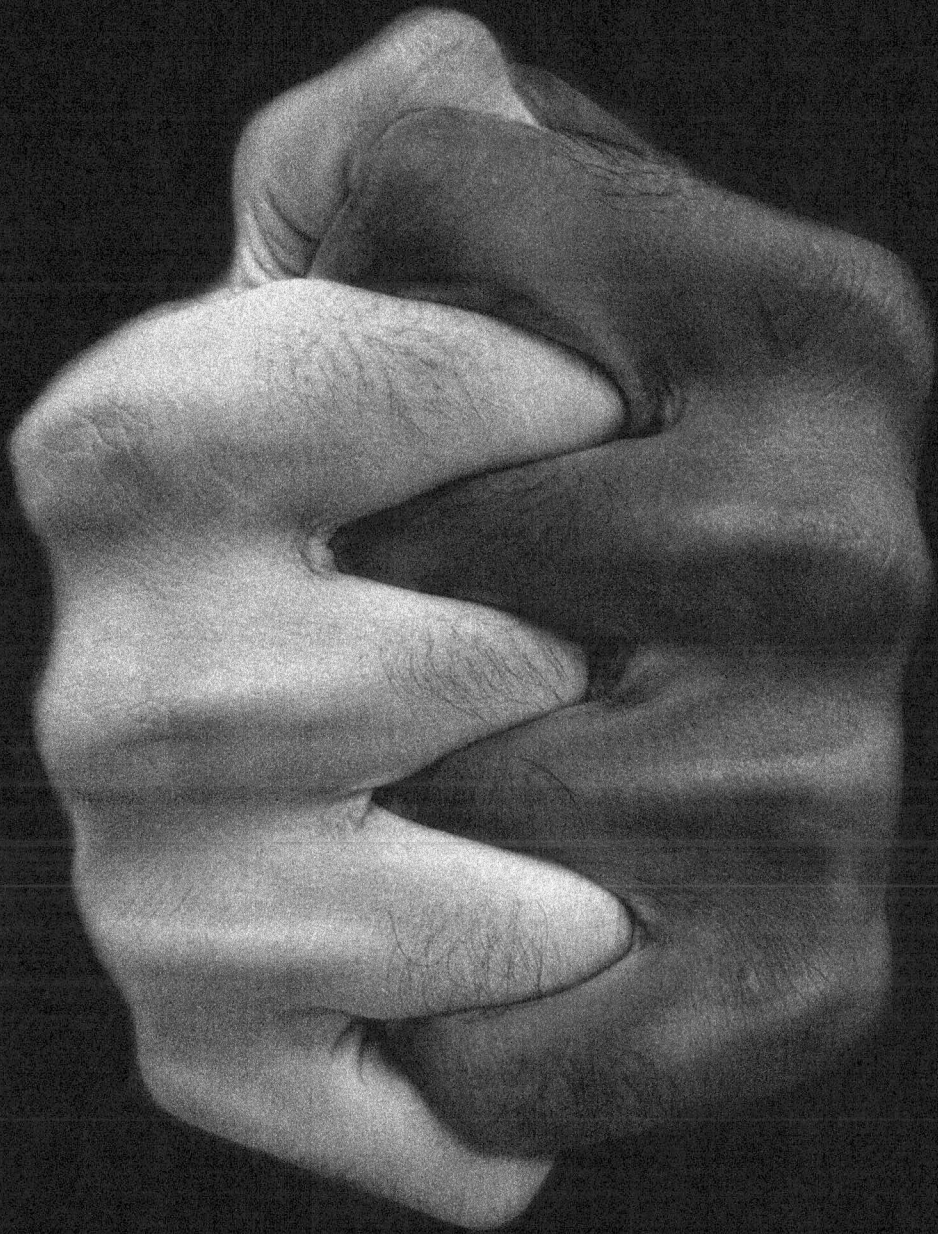

One of the most *damaging* behaviors in a relationship is not allowing a person to be *oneself*.

Our respect of human value should be *greater* than our material possessions.

OUR TIME AND FRIENDS ARE MORE VALUABLE THAN *GOLD*.

THE CAR YOU DRIVE,
SKIN COLOR,
THE SIZE OF YOUR HOUSE,
HAS *NOTHING* TO DO
WITH CHARACTER.

"Whoever walks in integrity walks securely..." Proverbs 10:9

Being *in love* and *loving* are two different matters.

The feeling of being in love is important, but the commitment of loving is greater.

If you want to know a person, don't interrupt them.

You'll learn more in silent observation than voicing your opinion.

Don't try to change a person, influence them. Live a life of excellence, transparency and honesty.

People will change by association or they will stay the same by separation.

TRUTH IS ALWAYS STRONGER THAN OPINION.

"And you will know the truth, and the truth will set you free."
John 8:32

Sometimes people will tell you more in *silence* than with words.

"The quiet words of the wise are more to be heeded than the shouts of a ruler of fools." Ecclesiastes 9:17

fo'c'sle ['fouksl] *n.* Nau: **1.** gaillard *m* pont de gaillard. **2.** (*in merchant vessel*) l'équipage.

focus¹, *pl.* **foci**, **focuses** ['fouk... 'foukəsiz] *n.* **1.** *Mth: Opt: etc: foyer m* etc.); *Opt:* **depth of f.,** (i) profondeur *f* profondeur de champ; **in f.,** (i) (*of im...* (ii) (*of instrument*) réglé; **out of f.,** (i) ...

When we don't give up, we *automatically* move ahead of failure.

SMALL THINKERS PUT YOU DOWN BUT BIG THINKERS LIFT YOU UP.

About the Author

J NORBERT McDANIEL has been involved in ministry for over 40 years, serving in a variety of areas. His servant heart and prophetic mantle, coupled with his strong evangelistic call, has opened doors to share the gospel domestically and abroad, including the countries of France, Italy, Great Britain, Belgium and Austria. Following is a summary of his past ministry involvement:

- Served as an Associate Pastor, overseeing intercessory prayer and outreach ministry, which included street and jail ministry teams.
- While an Assistant Pastor, served as an outreach evangelist.
- Worked with two major ministries.
- In addition to public ministry, served in local churches as a volunteer, participating in a variety of areas, including worship ministry teams as a drummer.

In addition to his ministry, he has been involved in managing two Christian-based seniors' complexes (a four-story independent living center and a 13-story senior facility).

Norbert has attended Oral Roberts University, C.H. Mason University and Next Dimension University. He resides in California.

Discover more about here:

JNORBERTMCDANIEL.ORG